BIG-NOTE PIANO

Best of Sara Bareilles

ISBN 978-1-4803-5307-7

HAL•LEONARD®
CORPORATION

7777 W. BLUEMOUND RD. P.O. BOX 13819 MILWAUKEE, WI 53213

Visit Hal Leonard Online at
www.halleonard.com

BRAVE

Words and Music by SARA BAREILLES
and JACK ANTONOFF

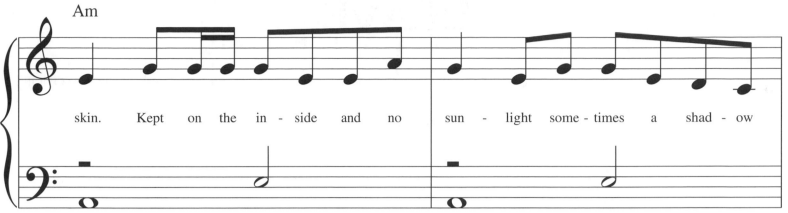

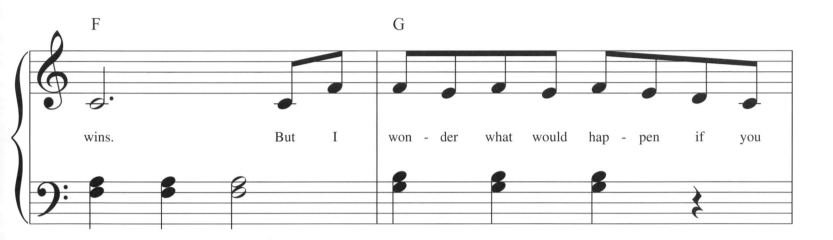

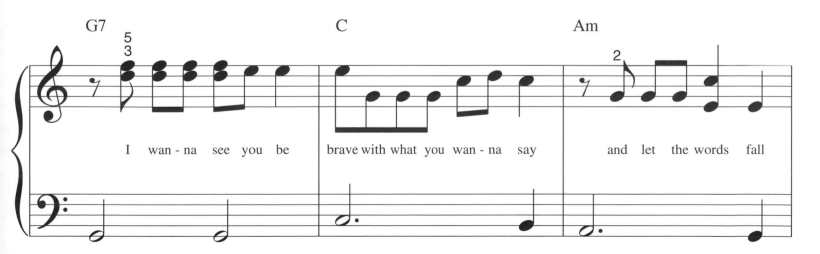

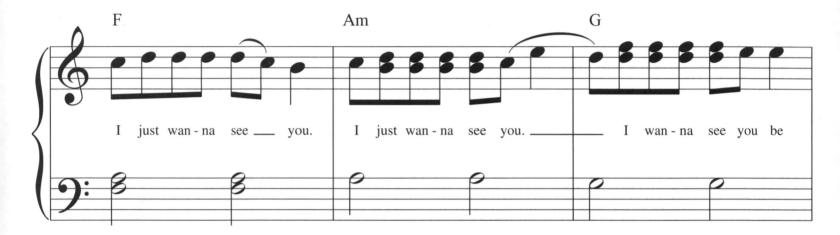

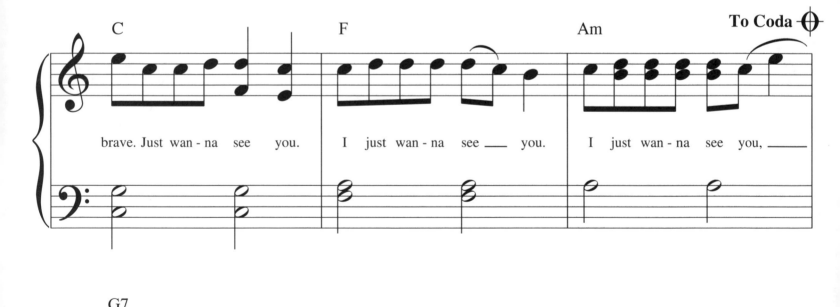

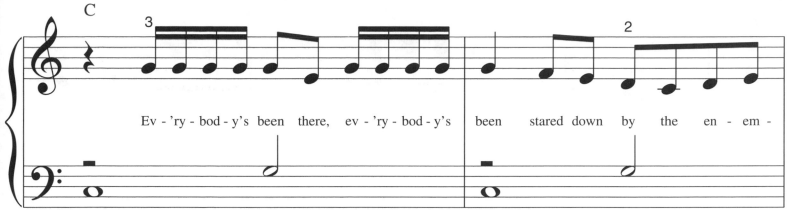

Ev - 'ry - bod - y's been there, ev - 'ry - bod - y's been stared down by the en - em -

y. Fall - en for the fear and done some dis - ap - pear - in', bow down to the might - y.

Don't run, just stop hold - in' your tongue. May - be there's a way

out of the cage where you live. May - be one of these days __ you can let the light __

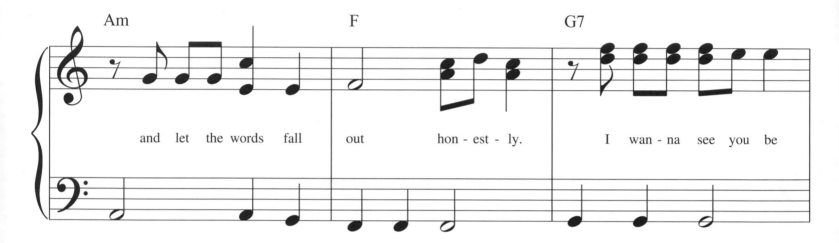

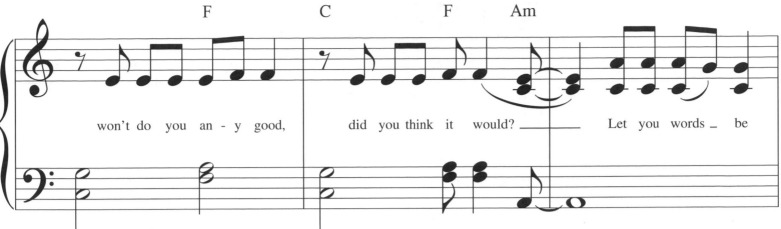

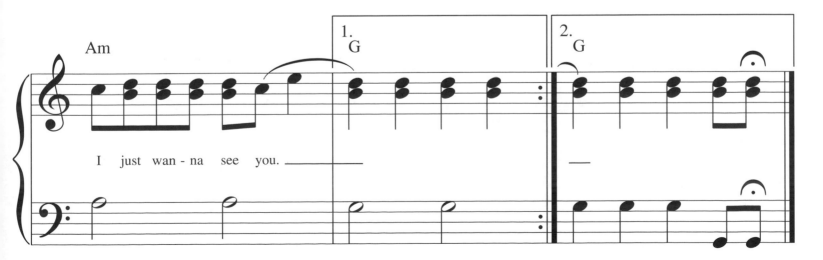

BOTTLE IT UP

Words and Music by
SARA BAREILLES

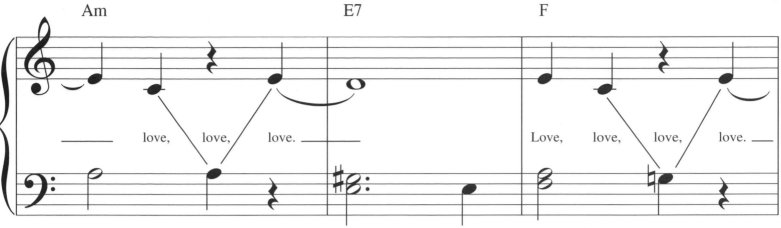

Am ... E7 ... F

_____ love, love, love. _____ Love, love, love, love. _____

C ... G/B ... Am

_____ I am aim - ing to be some - bod - y this
un - der - stand the sen - ti - ment you're

E7 ... F

some - bod - y trusts _____ with her del - i - cate soul. _____ I don't
say - ing to us. _____ Oh, but sen - si - ble sells, _____ so could you

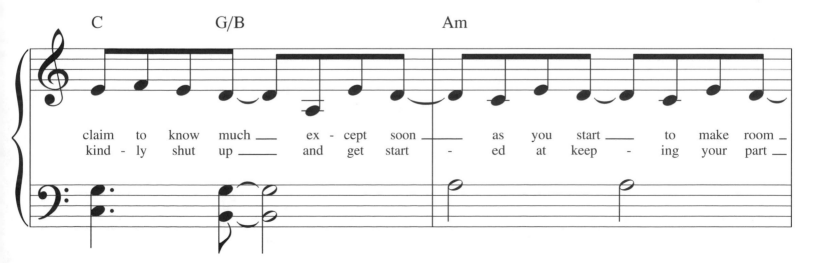

C ... G/B ... Am

claim to know much _____ ex - cept soon _____ as you start _____ to make room _____
kind - ly shut up _____ and get start - ed at keep - ing your part _____

for the parts ____ that aren't you, ____ it gets hard - er to
of the bar - gain. Aw, please, ____ lit - tle dar - lin', you're

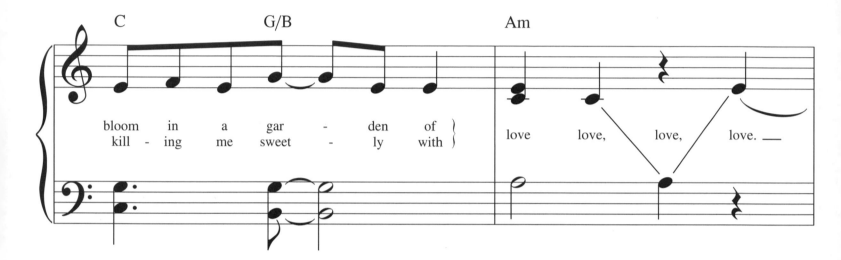

bloom in a gar - den of
kill - ing me sweet - ly with

love love, love, love. ____

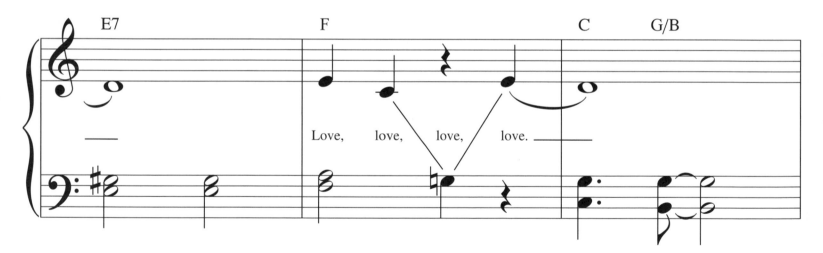

Love, love, love, love. ____

On - ly thing I ev - er could need, ____ on - ly one good thing worth

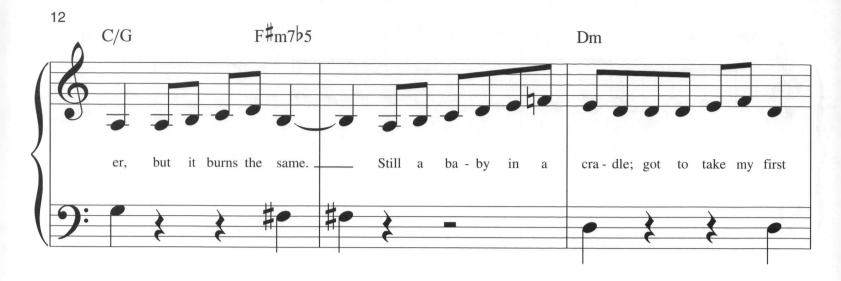

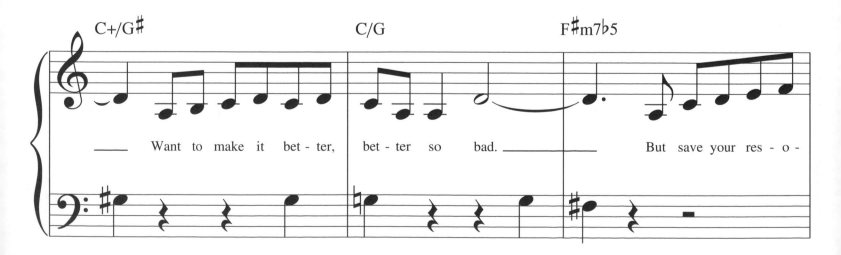

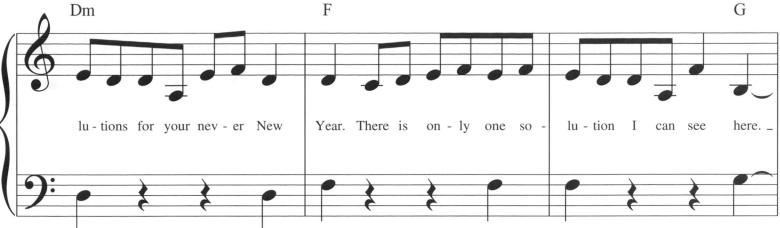

Dm   F   G

lu - tions for your nev - er New   Year. There is on - ly one so -   lu - tion I can see here. _

Am   C+/G♯

_   Love, you're all I   ev - er could need. _ On - ly

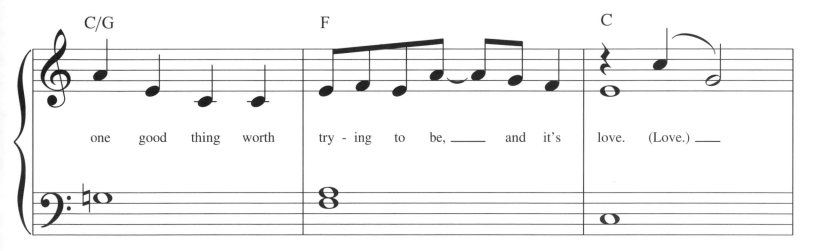

C/G   F   C

one good thing worth   try - ing to be, ___ and it's   love. (Love.) ___

G/B   Am   F

love, (Love.) ___   love, (Love.) _____   love. I do it for

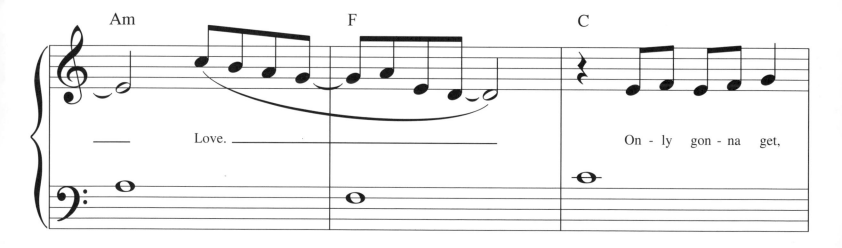

GONNA GET OVER YOU

Words and Music by SARA BAREILLES
and SAM FARRAR

I've got a thick tongue _____ brim-ming with the words that go

un - sung. _____ I sim - mer then I burn _____ for a some - one, _____

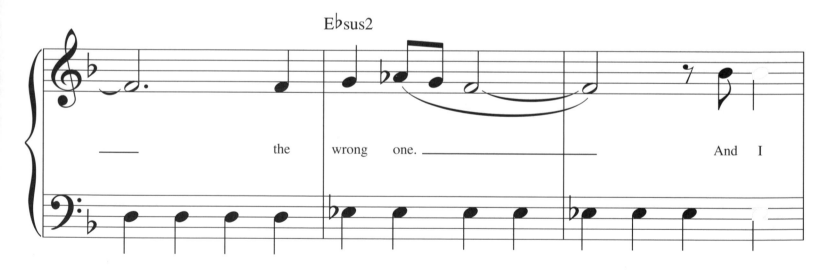

_____ the wrong one. _____ And I

tell my - self ____ to let ____ the sto - ry end, oh, ____

that my heart will rest ___ in some-one else ___'s

hand. ___ But my "why not ___ me" ___ phi-

los - o phy ___ be - gan. And I ___ said...

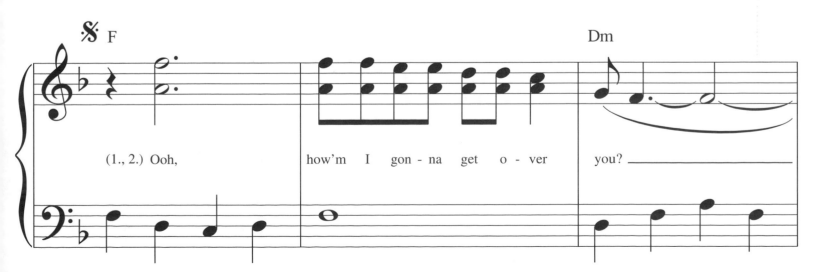

(1., 2.) Ooh, how'm I gon - na get o - ver you? ___

I'll ___ be ___ all right, _____ just ___

not to - night, but some - day.

Oh, I wish you'd want me to stay. _____ I'll ___ be

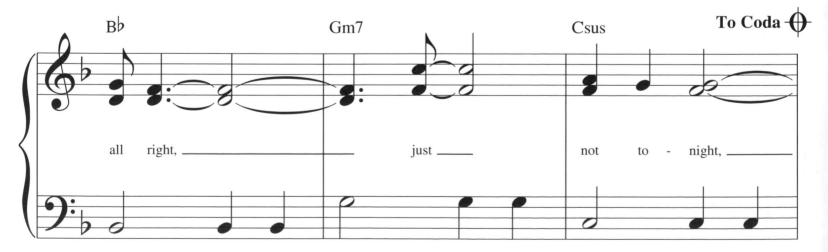

all right, _____ just ___ not to - night,

To Coda ⊕

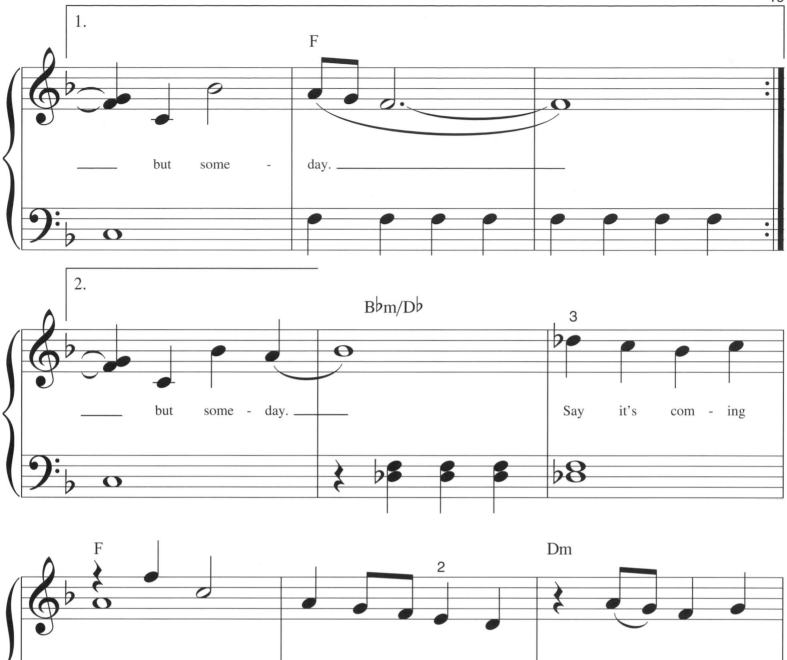

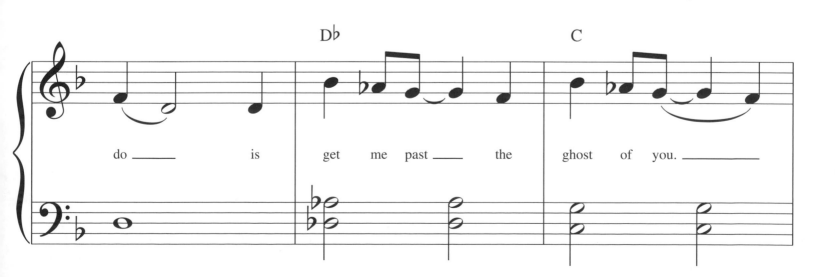

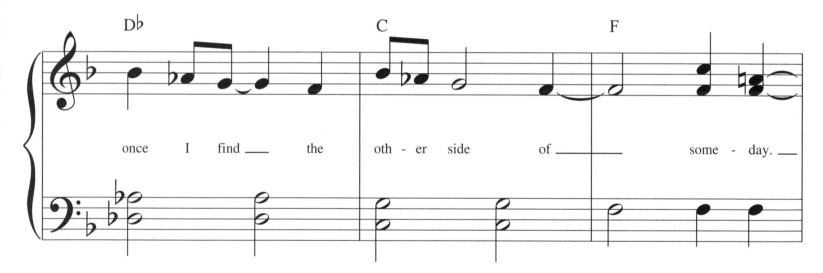

oh,   oh,   oh,

D.S. al Coda

CODA

whoa.

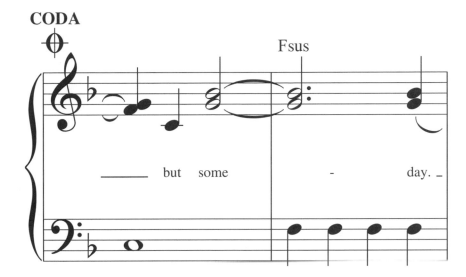

but some   -   day.

Additional Lyrics

2. "Maybe." It's a vicious little word that can
   Slay me, keep me where I'm hurting.
   You make me hang from your hands.
   But no more; I won't
   Beg to buy a shot at your back door.
   If I'm aching at the thought of you,
   What for? That's not me anymore.

   And I'm not the girl that I intend to be.
   But I dare you, darlin' just you wait and see.
   But this time not for you, but just for me.
   I said...

GRAVITY

Words and Music by
SARA BAREILLES

Moderately

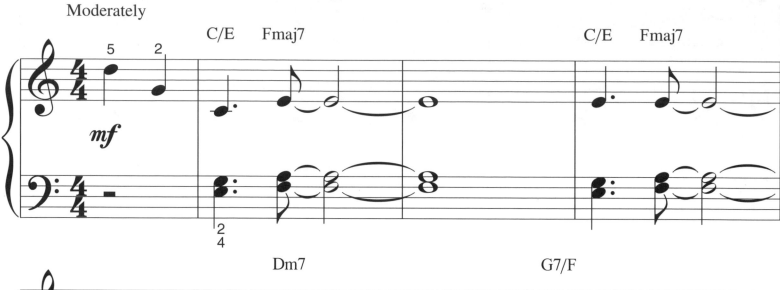

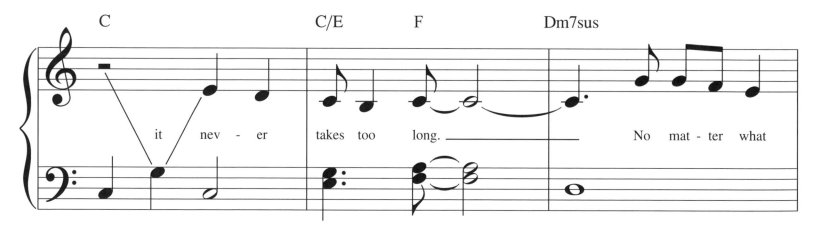

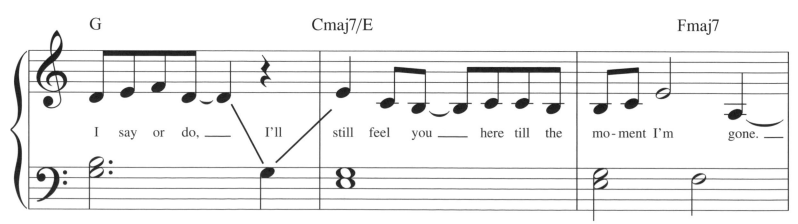

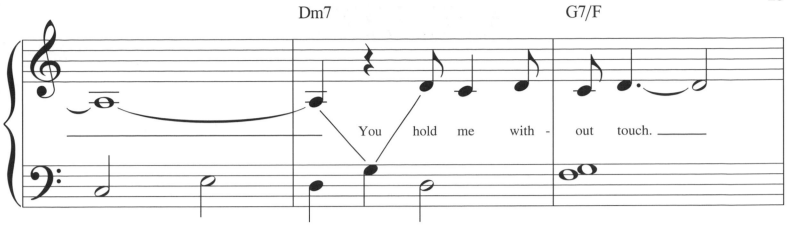

Dm7   G7/F

You hold me with-out touch. _____

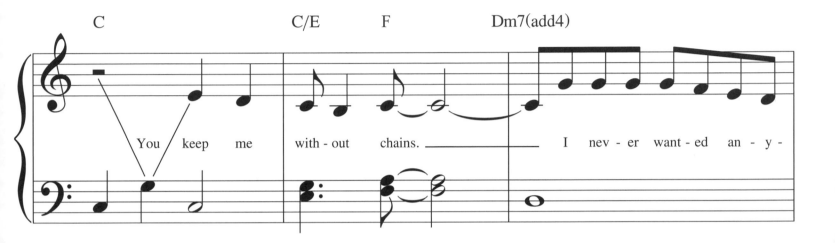

C   C/E   F   Dm7(add4)

You keep me with-out chains. _____ I nev-er want-ed an-y-

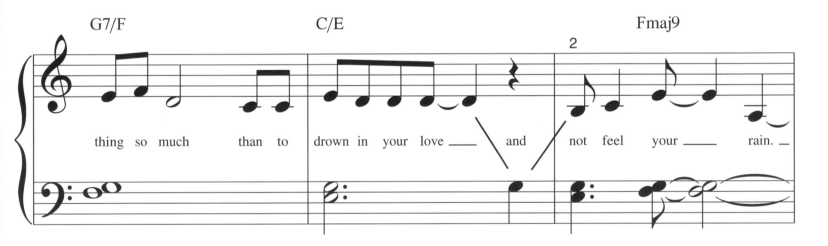

G7/F   C/E   Fmaj9
                                               2

thing so much than to drown in your love _____ and not feel your _____ rain. _____

Dm7   G7

Set _____ me free, _____ leave _____ me be. I don't wan-na

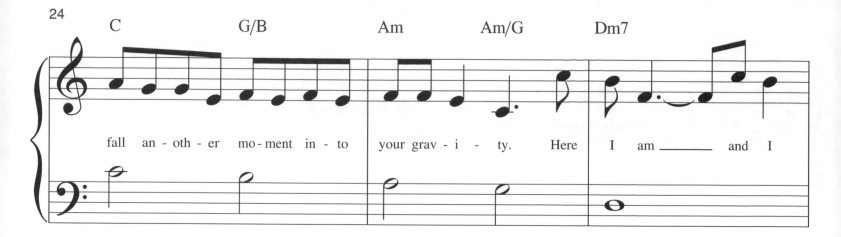

fall an - oth - er mo - ment in - to your grav - i - ty. Here I am _____ and I

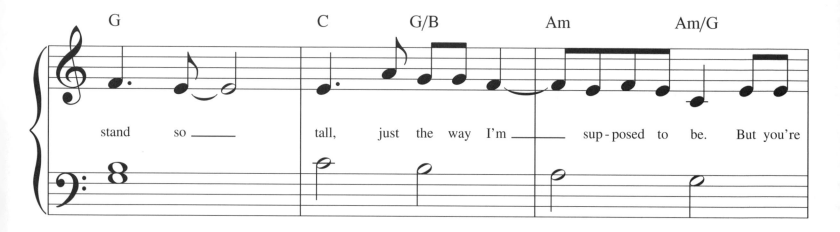

stand so _____ tall, just the way I'm _____ sup - posed to be. But you're

To Coda ⊕

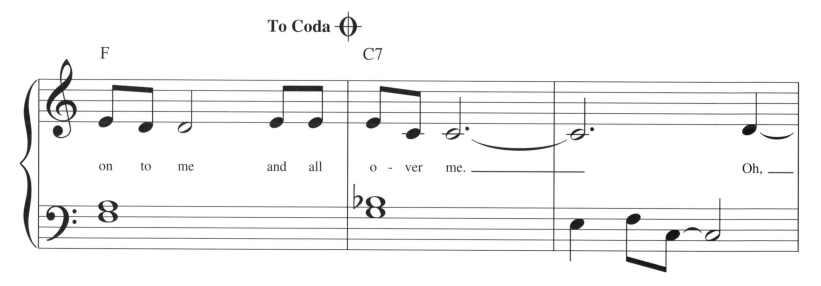

on to me and all o - ver me. _____ Oh, _____

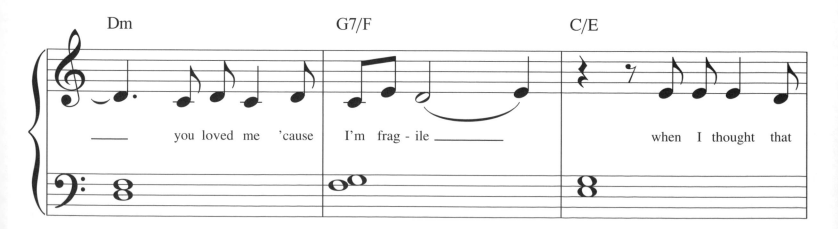

_____ you loved me 'cause I'm frag - ile _____ when I thought that

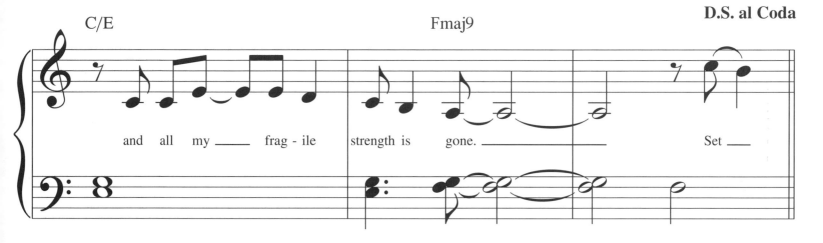

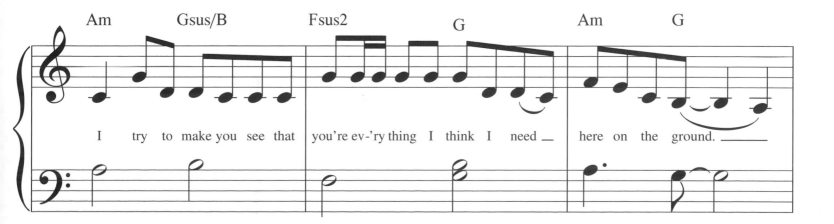

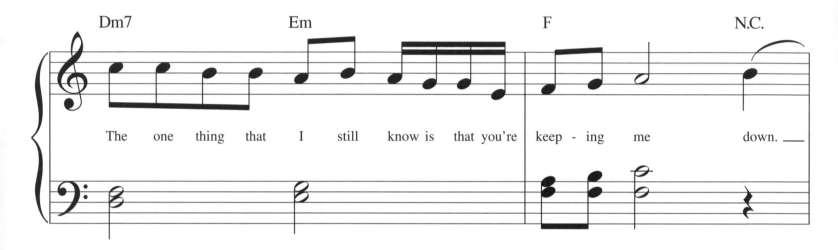

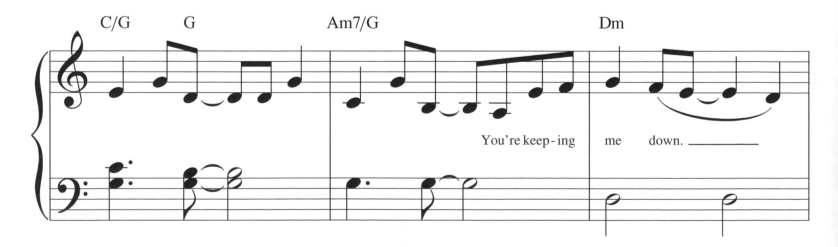

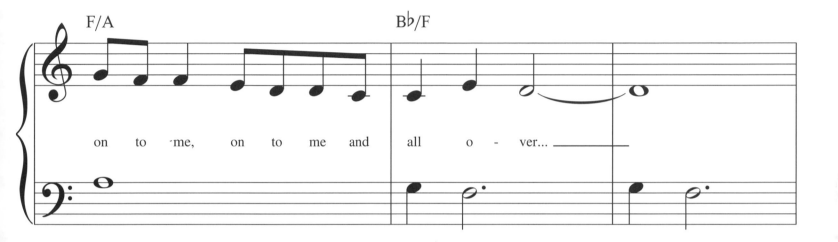

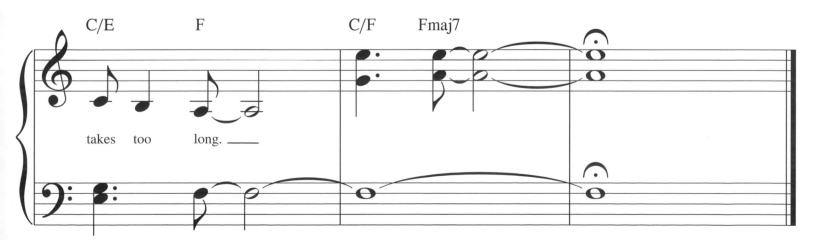

KING OF ANYTHING

Words and Music by
SARA BAREILLES

Moderately fast

Keep drink-ing cof-fee, stare me down a-cross the ta - ble

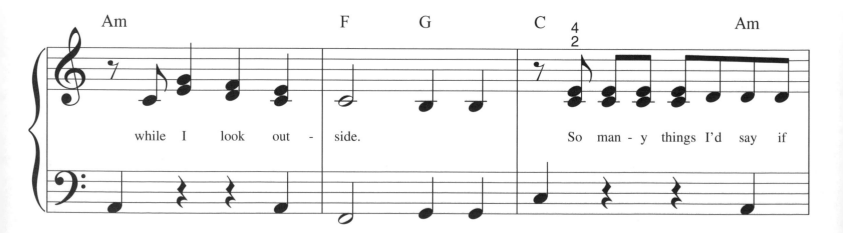

while I look out - side. So man - y things I'd say if

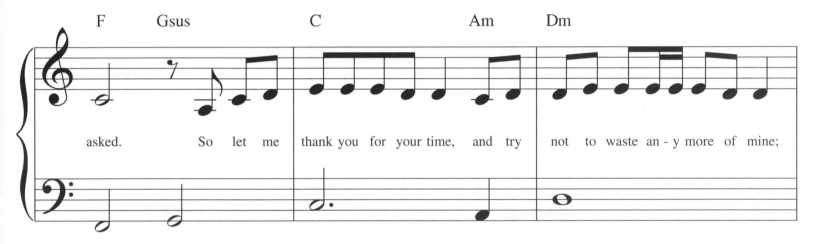

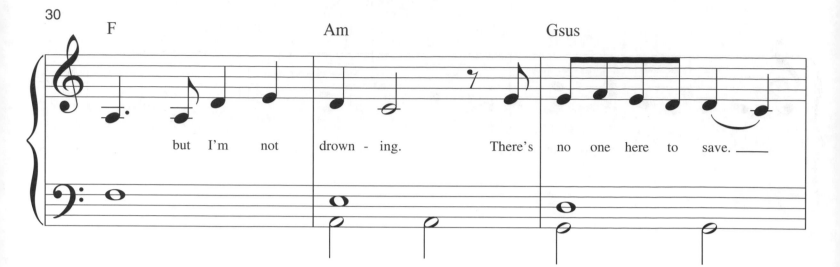

but I'm not drown - ing. There's no one here to save. ____

Who cares ____ if you dis - a - gree? You are not me. Who made you king ____

____ of an - y - thing? So you dare ____ tell me who ____ to be? Who

To Coda ⊕

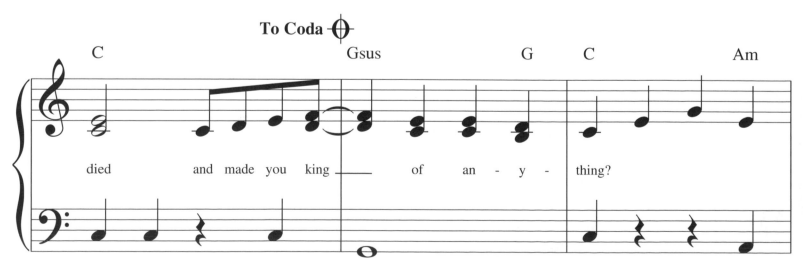

died and made you king ____ of an - y - thing?

You sound so in - no - cent, all full of good in - tent; swear you know

best. But you ex - pect me to jump up on board with you and ride

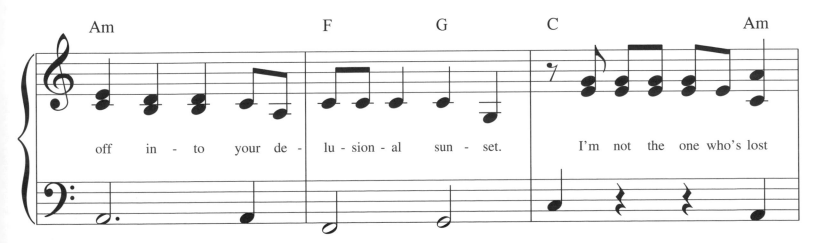

off in - to your de - lu - sion - al sun - set. I'm not the one who's lost

with no di - rec - tion, oh, but you'll nev - er see. You're so

bus - y mak - ing maps ___ with my name on them in all caps. You got the talk - ing down,

D.S. al Coda

CODA

just not the lis - ten - ing. ___ of an - y - thing? ___ All my

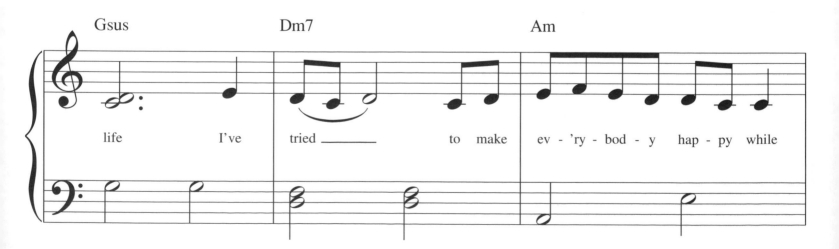

life I've tried ___ to make ev - 'ry - bod - y hap - py while

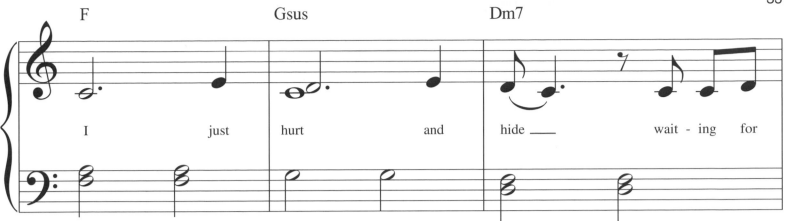

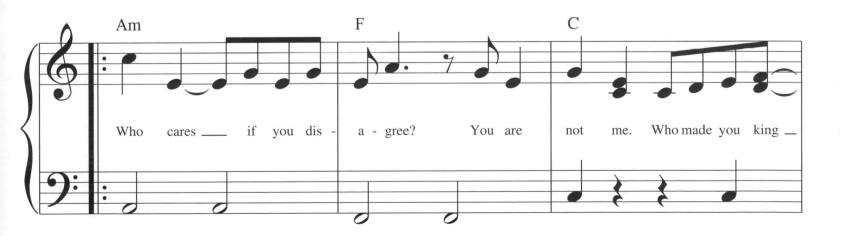

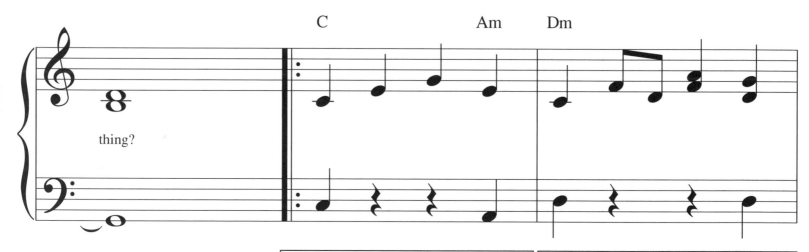

MANHATTAN

Words and Music by
SARA BAREILLES

And I'll tip - toe a - way   so you won't have to say

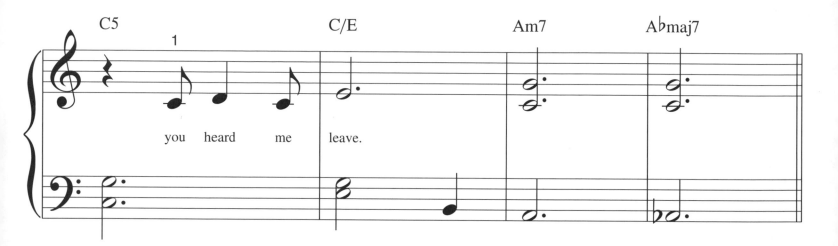

you heard me leave.

1. You can have Man - hat - tan; _____ I   know it's what _____ you   want;   the
2. *(See additional lyrics)*

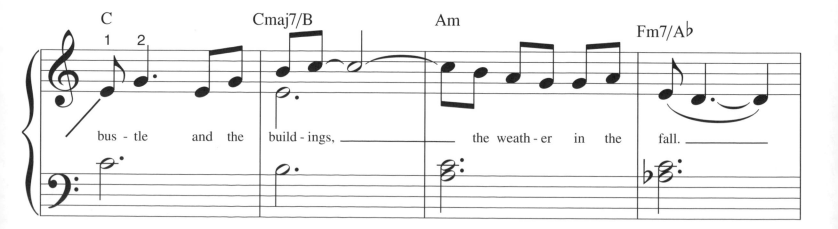

bus - tle and the build - ings, _____ _____ the weath - er in the fall. _____

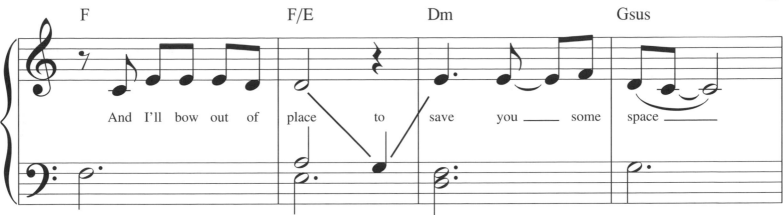

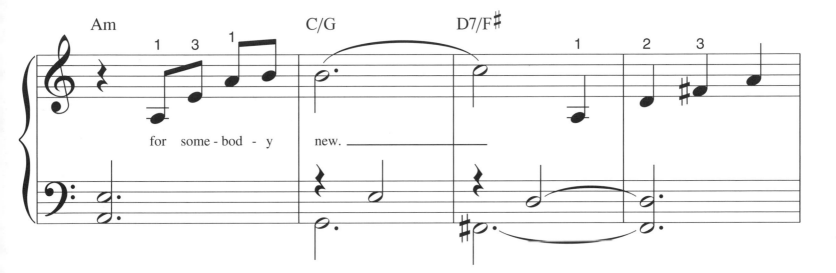

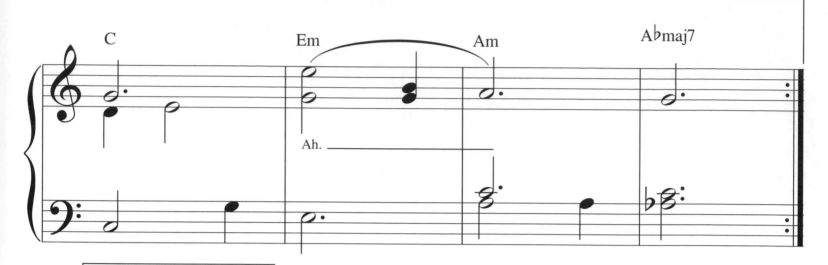

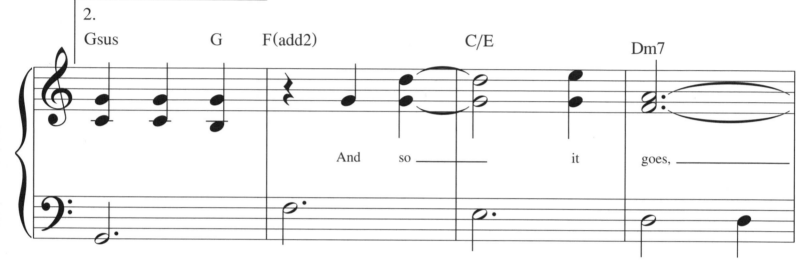

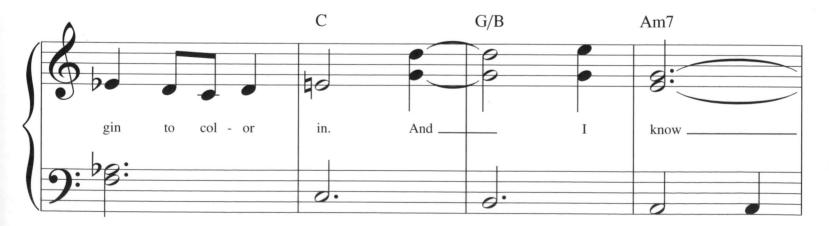

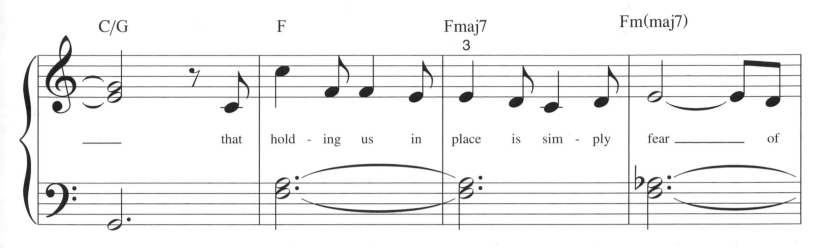

that hold - ing us in place is sim - ply fear _____ of

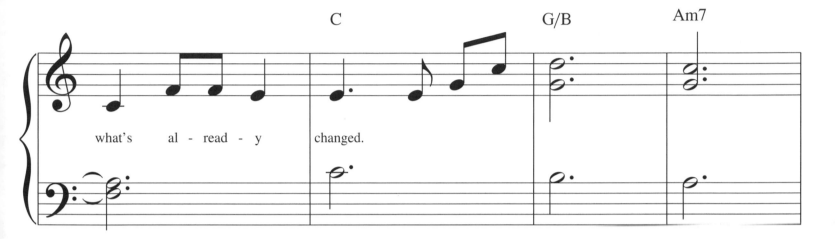

what's al - read - y changed.

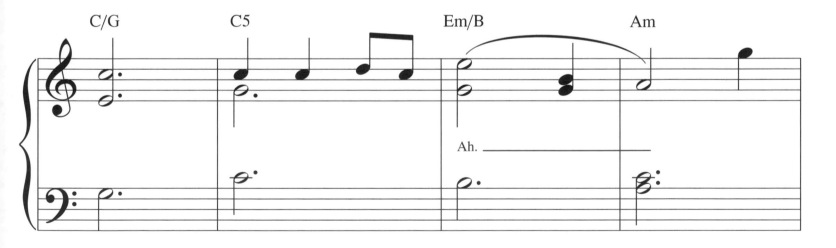

Ah. _____

You can have Man - hat - tan; _____ I'll set - tle for the

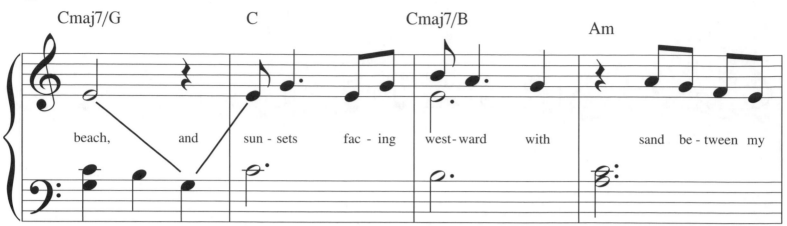

beach, and sun - sets fac - ing west-ward with sand be - tween my

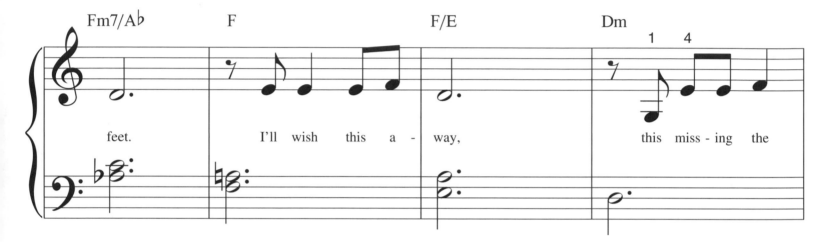

feet. I'll wish this a - way, this miss - ing the

days when I was one half of two.

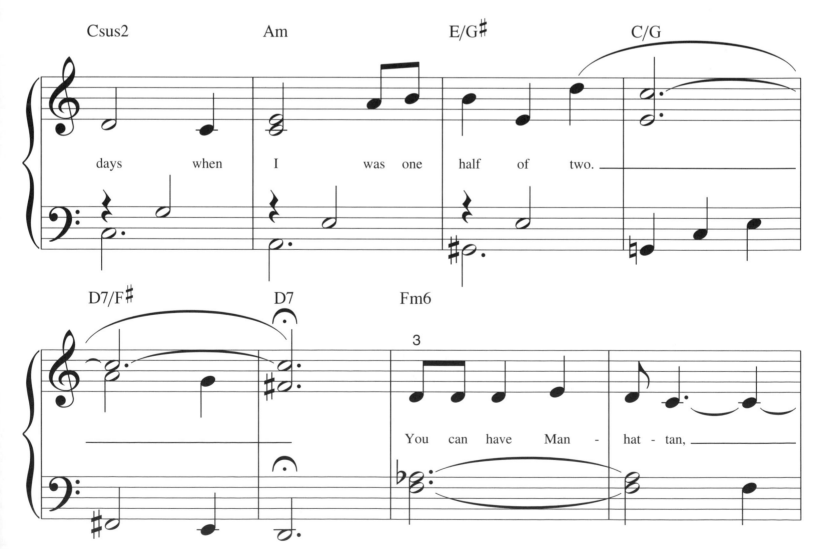

You can have Man - hat - tan,

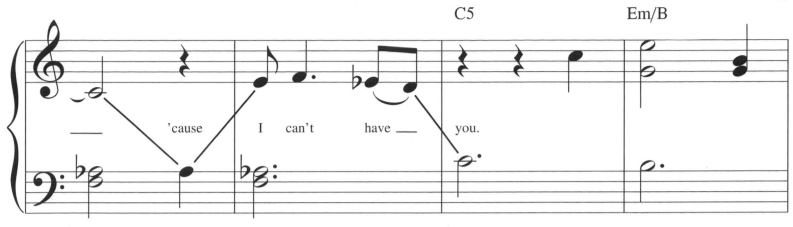

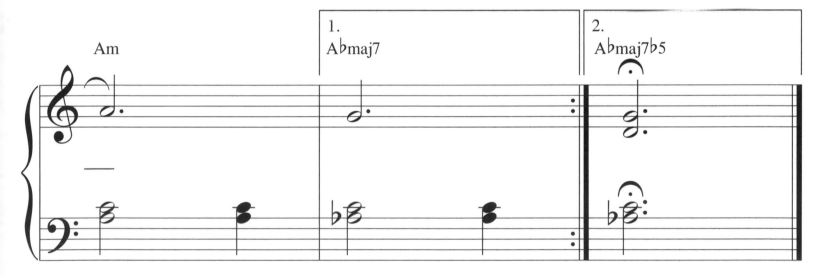

Additional Lyrics

2. You can have Manhattan,
   The one we used to share,
   The one where we were laughing
   And drunk on just being there.
   Hang on to the reverie;
   Could you do that for me?
   'Cause I'm just too sad to.
   You can have Manhattan
   'Cause I can't have you.

LOVE SONG

Words and Music by
SARA BAREILLES

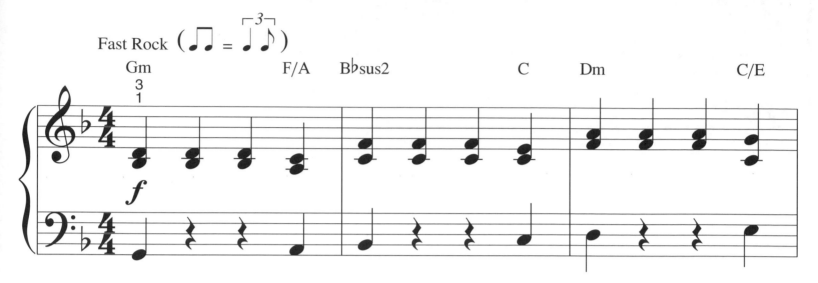

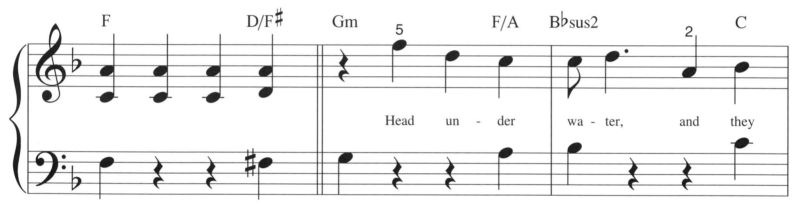

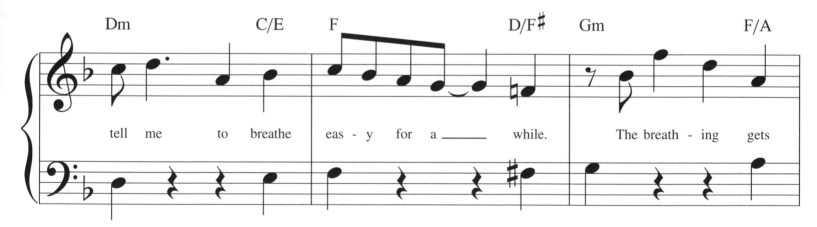

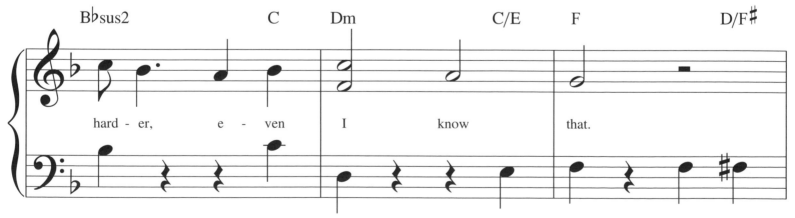

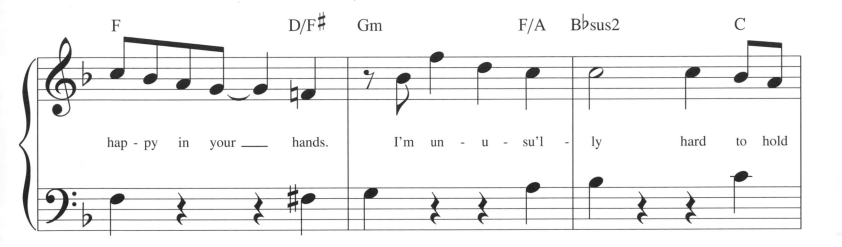

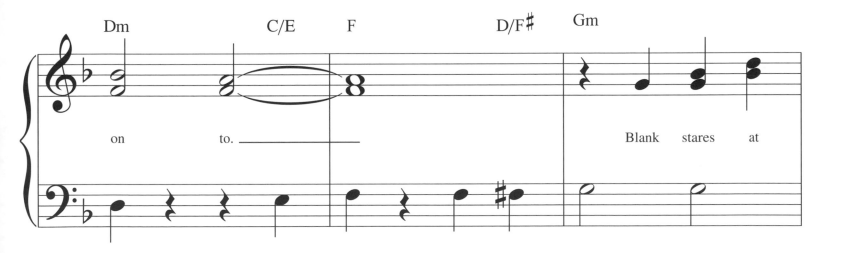

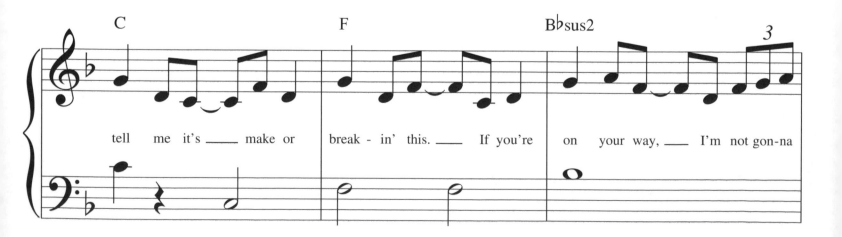

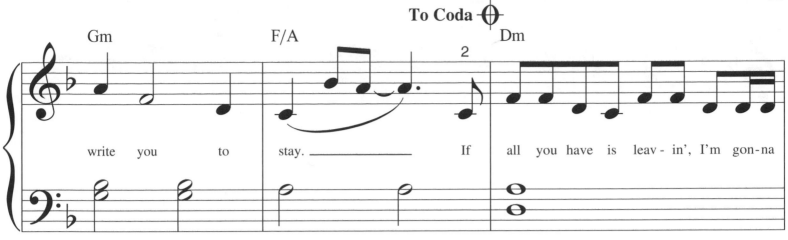

write you to stay. _____ If all you have is leav - in', I'm gon-na

need a bet - ter rea - son to write you a love song to -

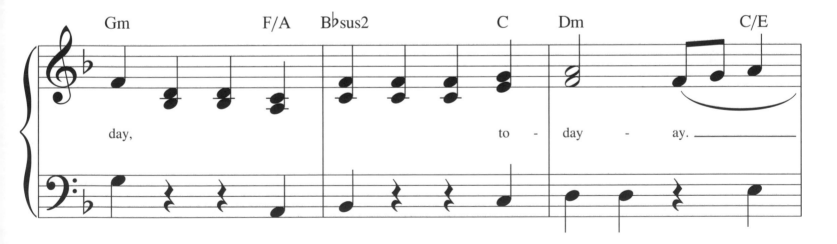

day, to - day - ay. _____

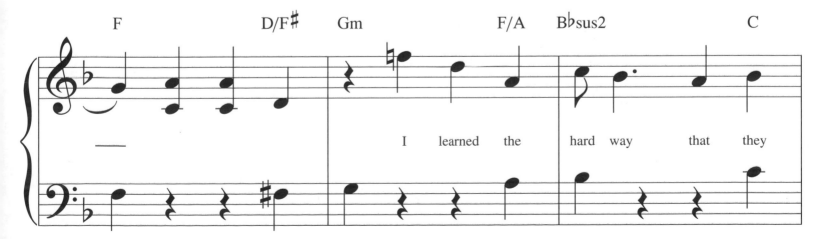

_____ I learned the hard way that they

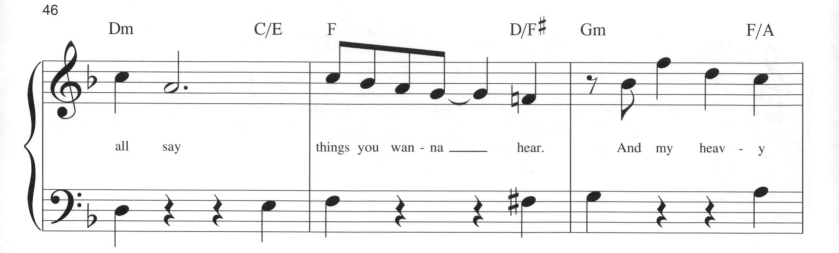

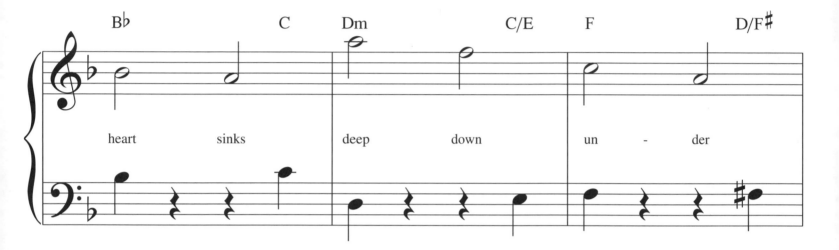

Dm   C/E   F   D/F♯   Gm

high   and   dry.   Con - vinced me

F/A   B♭sus2   C   D/A

to please you.   Made me think   that I need this

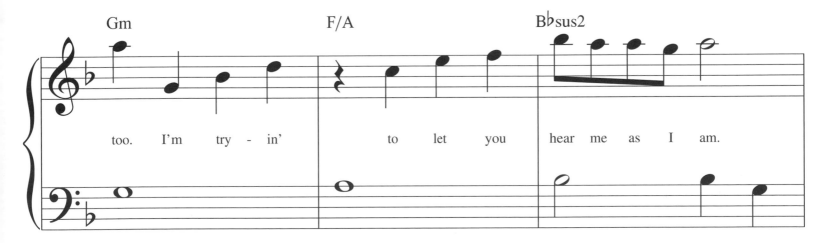

Gm   F/A   B♭sus2

too. I'm try - in'   to let you   hear me as I am.

D.S. al Coda

CODA

Dm

I'm not gon-na write you a

all you have is leav- in', I'm gon-na

need a bet - ter rea - son to write you _____ a love song _____ to -

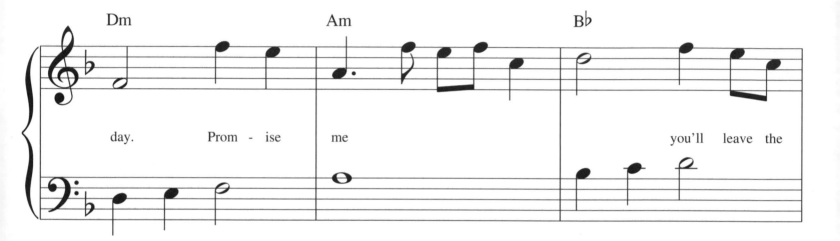

day. Prom - ise me you'll leave the

light on to help me see

the day - light. My guide, come on. _____ 'Cause I be - lieve _

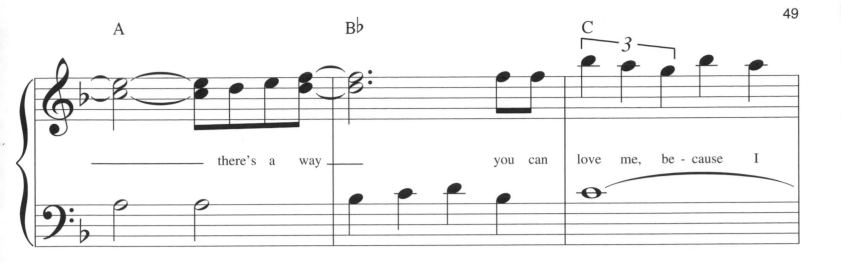

there's a way ___ you can love me, be-cause I

say I won't write you a love song ___ 'cause you ask ___ for it, ___ 'cause you

need one. ___ You see, I'm not gon-na write you a love song ___ 'cause you

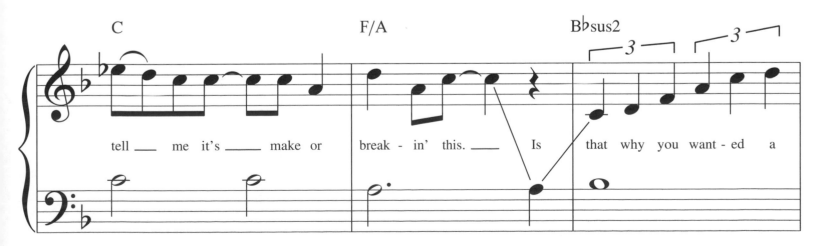

tell ___ me it's ___ make or break-in' this. ___ Is that why you want-ed a

50

walk the sev - en seas when I be - lieve that there's a rea - son to write you _____ a

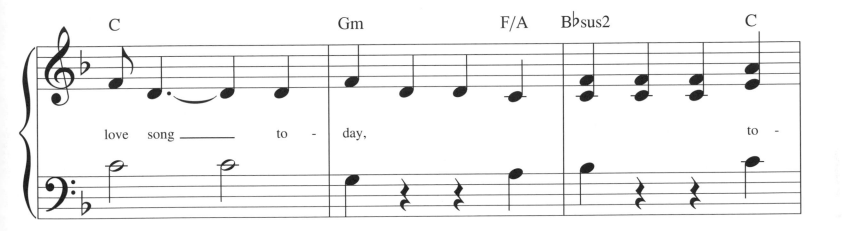

love song _____ to - day, to -

day.

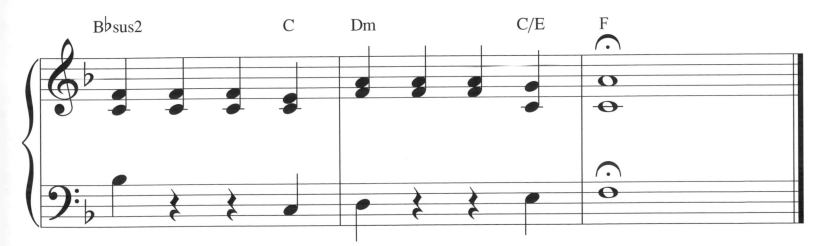

STAY

Words and Music by
SARA BAREILLES

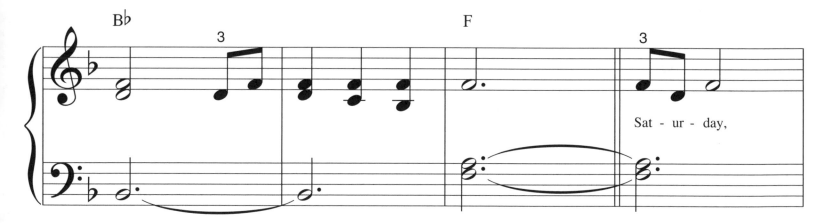

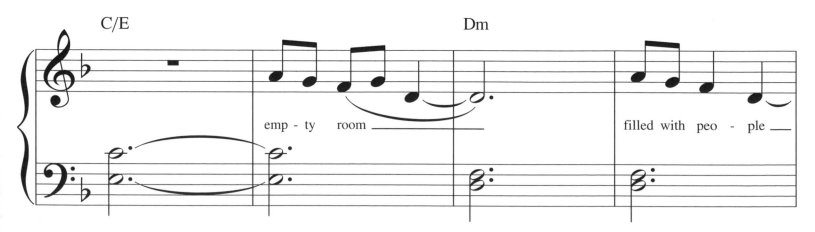

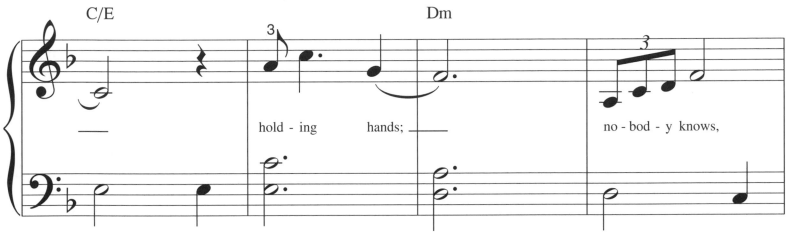

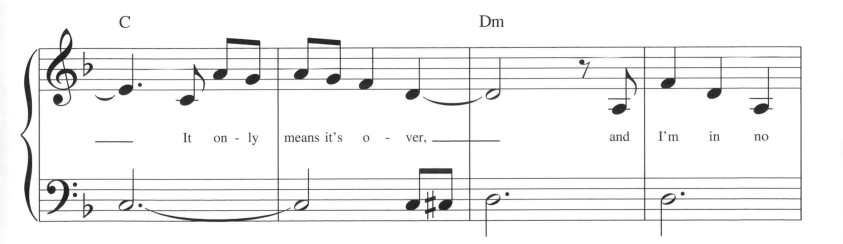

54

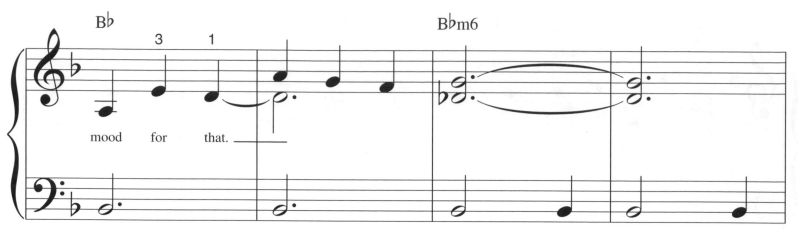

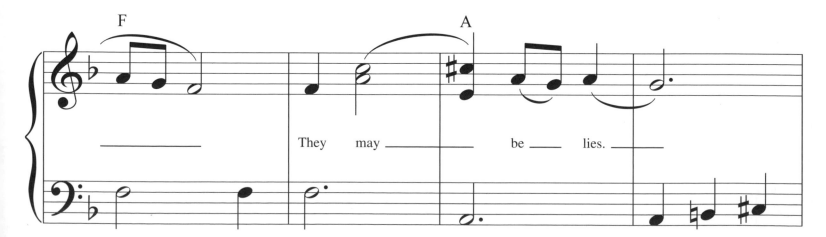

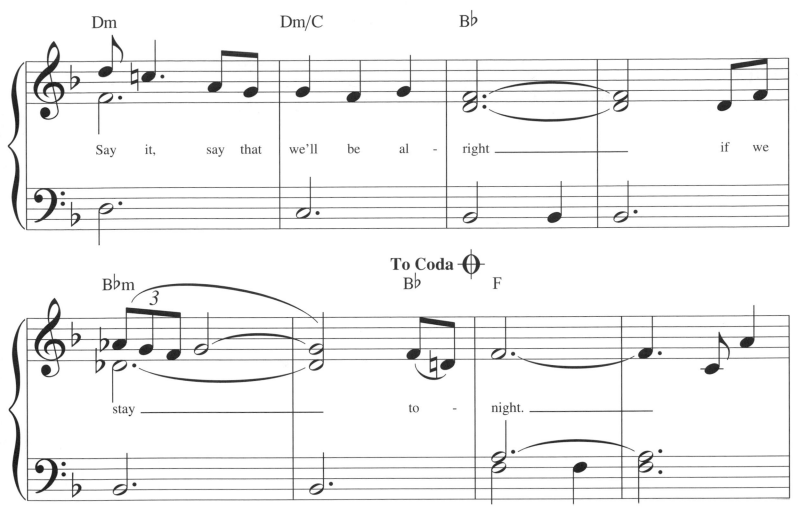

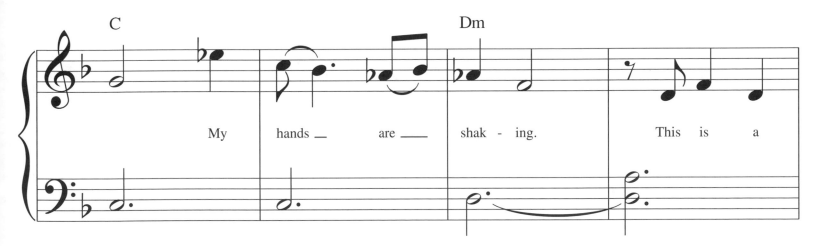

closed, _____ I've seen it, ba - by. I've seen where this

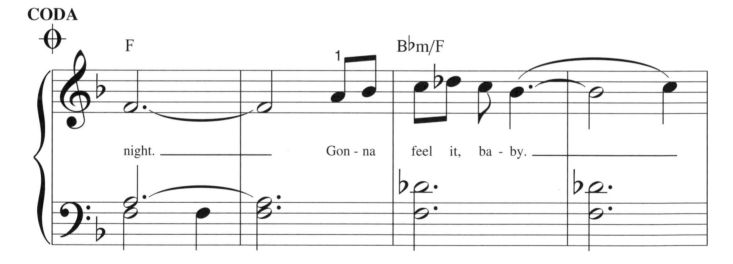

goes. _____ Oh. _____

D.S. al Coda

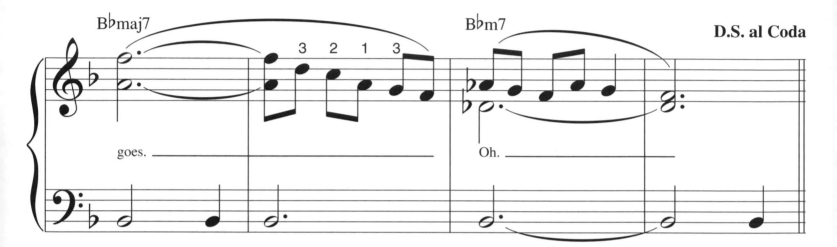

CODA

night. _____ Gon - na feel it, ba - by. _____

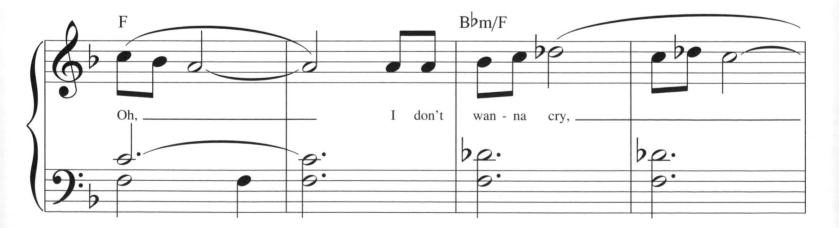

Oh, _____ I don't wan - na cry, _____

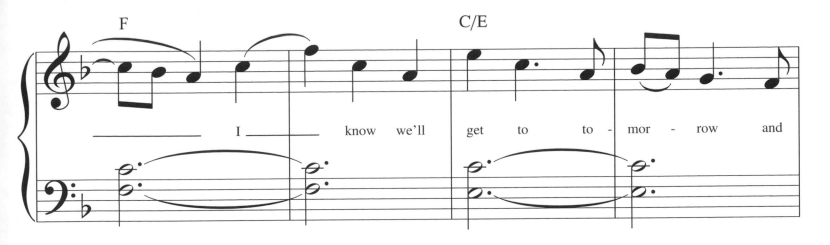

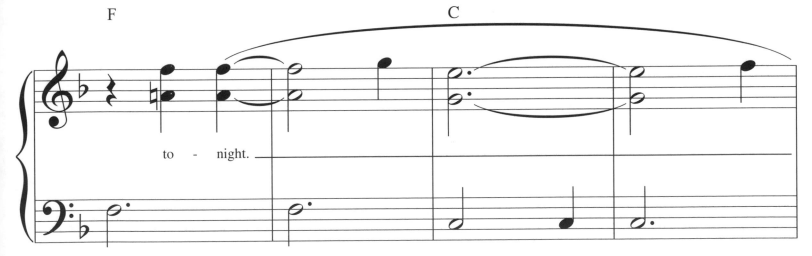

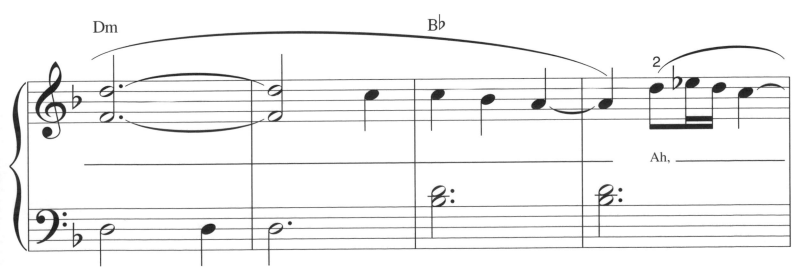

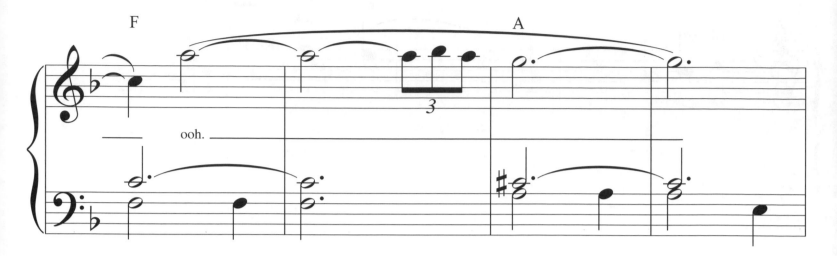

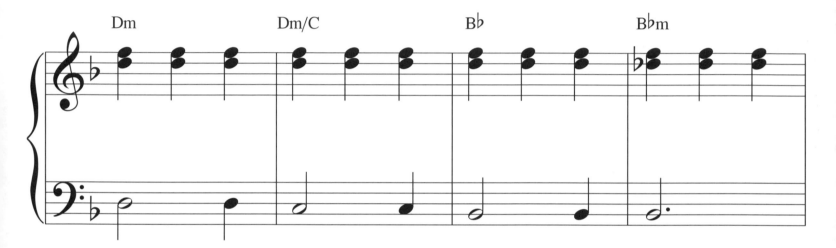

They may be lies.

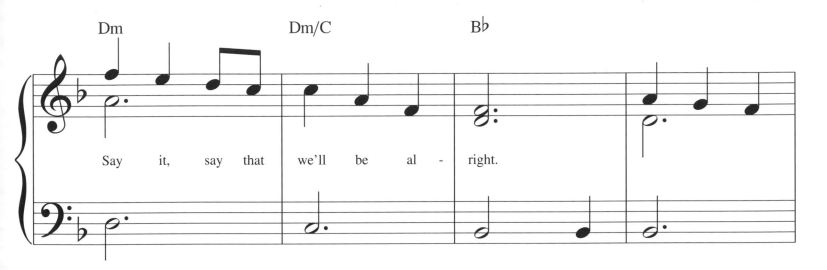

Say it, say that we'll be al - right.

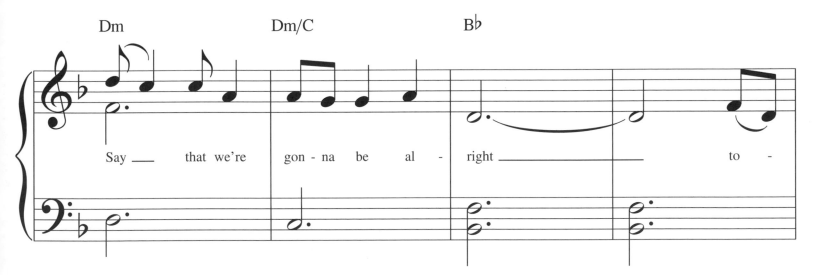

Say that we're gon - na be al - right to -

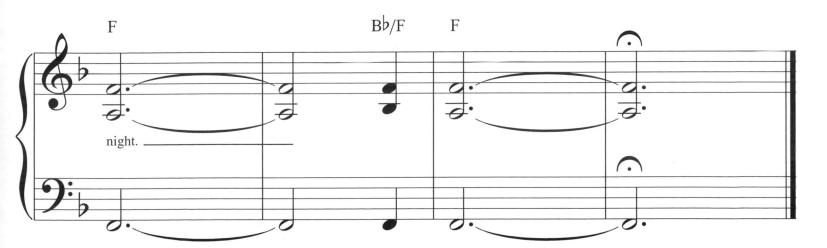

night.

UNCHARTED

Words and Music by
SARA BAREILLES

Moderately

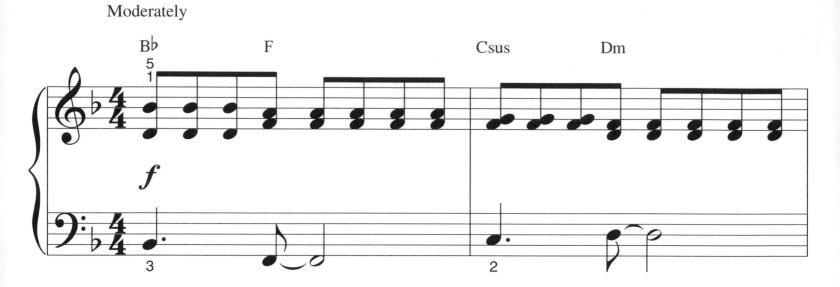

No words; ____ my tears won't make an - y room for 'em, oh, and it

don't hurt like an - y - thing I've ev - er felt be - fore. This is

no bro - ken heart, __ no fam - il - iar scars. __ This ter - ri - to - ry

goes un - chart - ed.

1. Just me in a room sunk down in a house in a town, and I
2. *(See additional lyrics)*

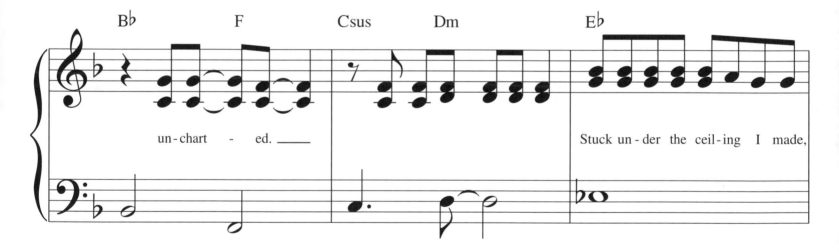

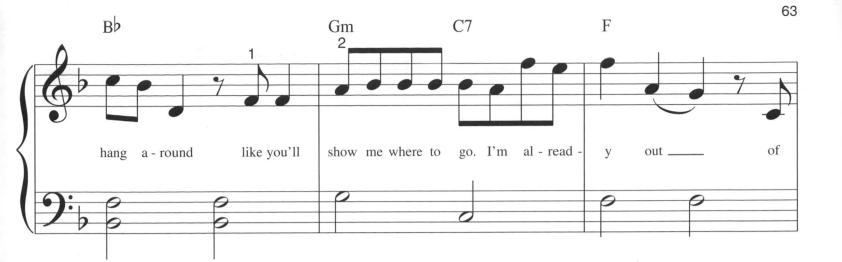

hang a-round like you'll show me where to go. I'm al-read-y out _____ of

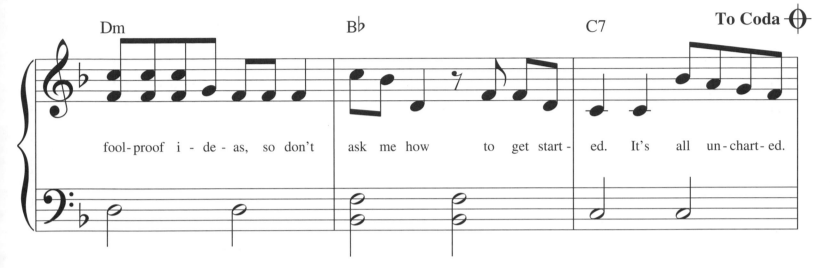

To Coda ⊕

fool-proof i-de-as, so don't ask me how to get start-ed. It's all un-chart-ed.

1.

La, la, la, la, ___ ah, oh. ___

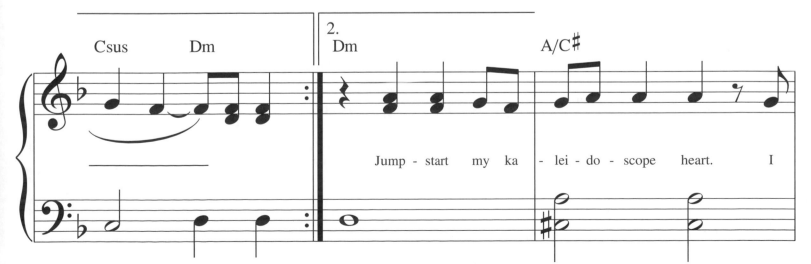

2.

_____ Jump-start my ka-lei-do-scope heart. I

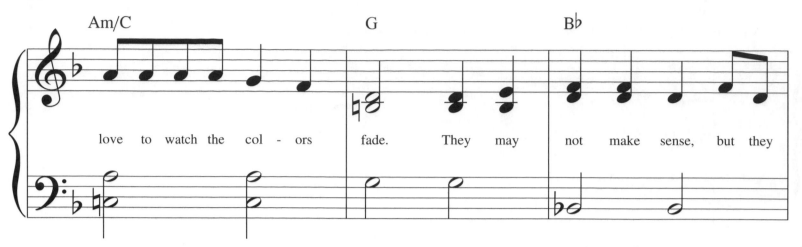

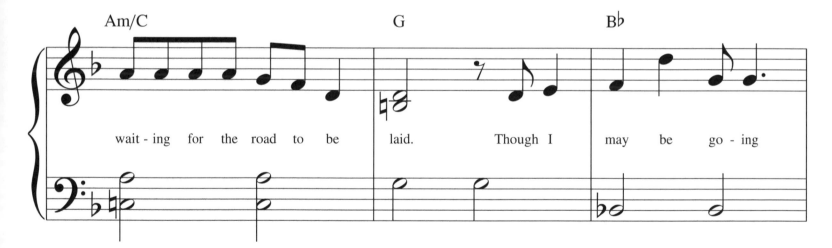

Com - pare where you are to where you want to be, and you'll get

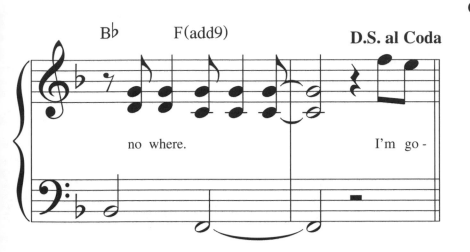

no where. I'm go-

Additional Lyrics

2. Each day I'm counting up the minutes till I
   Get alone 'cause I
   Can't stay in the middle of it all.
   It's nobody's fault, but I'm so low;
   Never knew how much I didn't know.
   Oh, ev'rything is uncharted.
   I know I'm getting nowhere when I
   Only sit and stare like
   I'm going down...

WINTER SONG

Words and Music by SARA BAREILLES
and INGRID MICHAELSON

Moderately slow

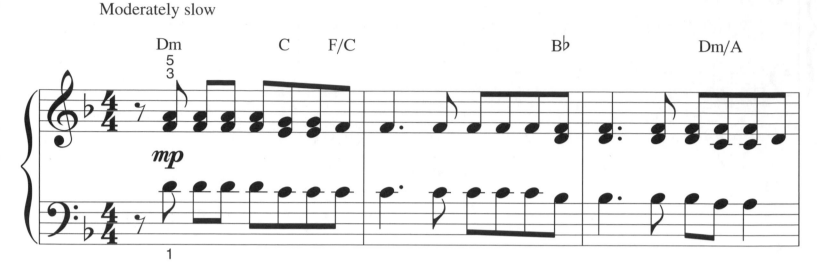

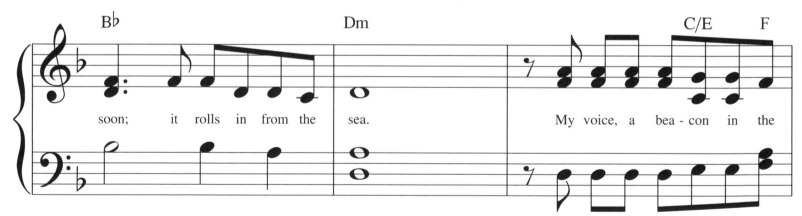

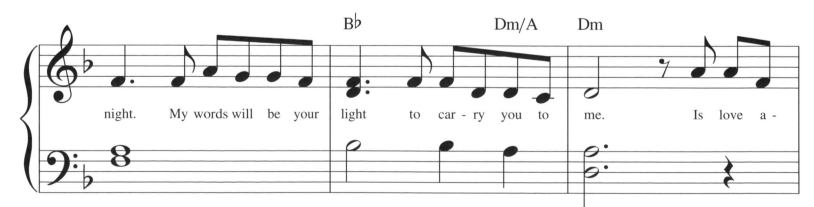

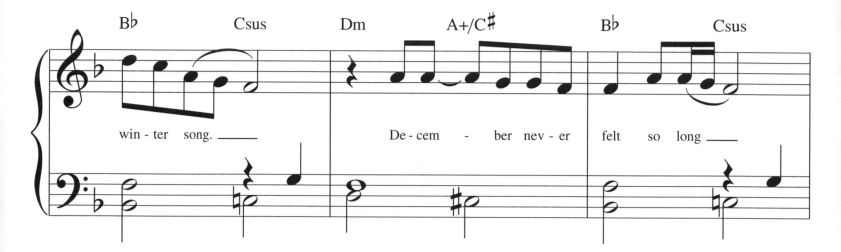

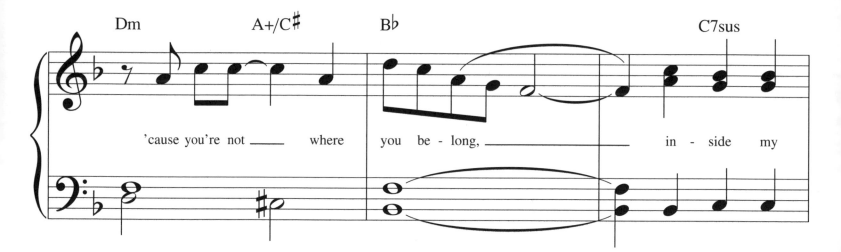

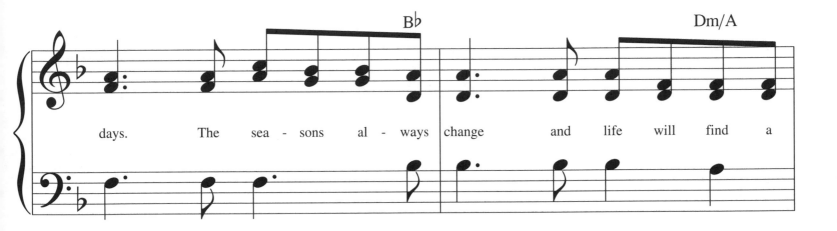

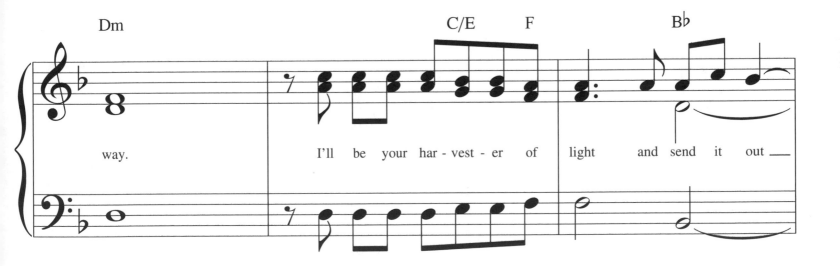

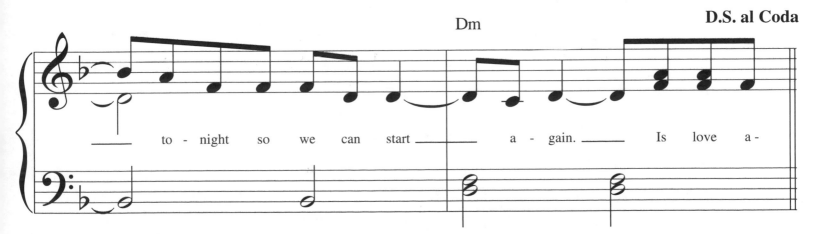

CODA

This is my win-ter song to you. The storm is com-ing soon; it rolls in from the

sea.   My love, a bea-con in the night.   My words will be your

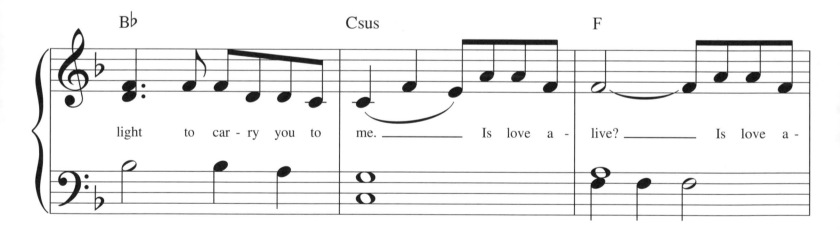

light   to car-ry you to me. _____ Is love a-live? _____ Is love a-

live? _____ Is love a-live? _____ Is love a-live? _____ Is love a-